ARSENAL
CONFIDENTIAL

D1147112

ARSENAL
CONFIDENTIAL

FOREWORD BY ARSÈNE WENGER

hamlyn

Produced for Hamlyn by **Flanders Publishing**

An **Hachette Livre UK Company**
www.hachettelivre.co.uk

First published in Great Britain in 2008 by
Hamlyn, a division of **Octopus Publishing Group Ltd**
2–4 Heron Quays, London E14 4JP
www.octopusbooks.co.uk

Copyright © Octopus Publishing Group Ltd 2008

ISBN 978-0-600-61890-4

A CIP catalogue record for this book is available
from the British Library

Printed and bound in Italy

10 9 8 7 6 5 4 3 2 1

Text by **Richard Clarke**
Pictures by **Stuart MacFarlane**
Executive Editor **Trevor Davies**
Project Editor **Julian Flanders**
Designer **Craig Stevens**
Production **Carolin Stransky**

CONTENTS

FOREWORD

The 2007/08 season was full of highs and lows as we challenged for honours on all four fronts. We had some memorable matches, with the victory against AC Milan at the San Siro standing out, and scored some wonderful goals. But what I was most pleased with was the attitude and determination of the players along with their desire to play entertaining football. I always thought that the team was capable of playing with high quality and could keep on improving, but ultimately we couldn't secure silverware last season. However, I feel that we are continuing to develop and can challenge for all four trophies again in 2008/09.

The images in this book give you, the supporter, a unique insight into the Club, from pre-season preparation to matchdays. They look behind-the-scenes to the Club at work and capture the extraordinary spirit that is evident within Arsenal Football Club.

I believe these images show what a special club Arsenal is and what potential there is for us to continue to grow. Everyone involved with the Club plays a special role in delivering success, including you – our supporters. The team spirit within this squad is fantastic, the players want to fight together and win together. These images also highlight the focus that the squad has in working together to achieve honours.

Arsenal Confidential captures the drama of the 2007/08 season and illustrates the true uniqueness of the Club: what I, the players and of course the fans, find special about it.

I hope you enjoy this pictorial journey through the season.

Arsène Wenger
Manager, Arsenal Football Club

PRE-SEASON

The Arsenal players normally return to training at the start of July each year. For the past six seasons their early work at London Colney has been followed by a 10-day training camp in Austria.

Arsène Wenger bases his side high in the hills of the Styria region. It is an isolated, peaceful environment and the perfect platform from which to take on the rigours of tough twice-daily sessions. The first takes place in mid-morning, the second in late afternoon. That way Wenger's men avoid the worst of the Austrian heat.

Normally, Arsenal play a couple of friendlies, sometimes against relatively low-level local opposition. But these games are not the main focus of the camp. It is about fitness, togetherness and preparation for the long season to come. It also helps integrate any summer signings into the Arsenal family.

The intensity of competition increases once the team leaves Austria. For example, in 2007 the inaugural Emirates Tournament saw Valencia, Paris St Germain and Inter Milan visit North London. Then Arsenal travelled to Holland for the Amsterdam Tournament in which they took on Ajax and Lazio.

This period is the foundation upon which the team's trophy charge will be built.

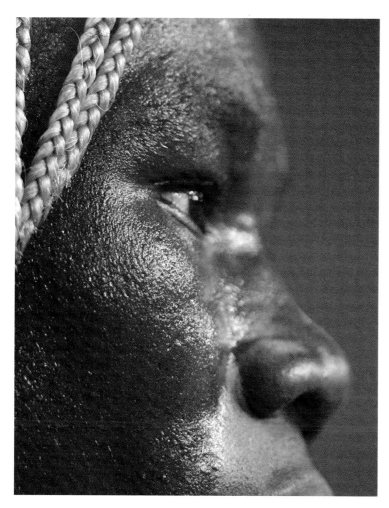

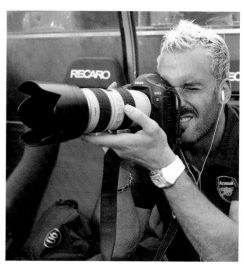

Opposite Arsène Wenger pitted his wits against Giovanni Trapattoni in July 2007. The legendary Italian manager was in charge of Red Bull Salzburg when Arsenal were invited to help open the redeveloped Bulls Arena. But the smile disappeared off Wenger's face at full time as the hosts won 1-0.

'At Auxerre we used to run
a lot during pre-season, at
Arsenal we use the ball more.
It is different but it is good.'

BACARY SAGNA

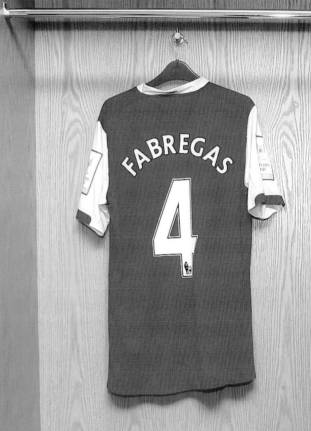

Every session in Austria ends with stretching.
It is crucial to look after players' muscles
during the intense twice-daily sessions.

'It is always good for team spirit to be together in pre-season. We are like a big family anyway but out here the players are really bouncy in the dressing room.'

THEO WALCOTT

'We play massive sides in Amsterdam. It is always good to compare yourself to the best in Europe ahead of the challenges in the Premier League.'

NICKLAS BENDTNER

Arsène Wenger does 'a little bit of fitness every day' to maintain his own health. In Austria, he normally spurns the team bus to training and cycles instead. It is only a short journey but it does mean going up and down a very steep hill twice a day.

'The team suffered during last season but suffering makes you more mature.'

ARSÈNE WENGER

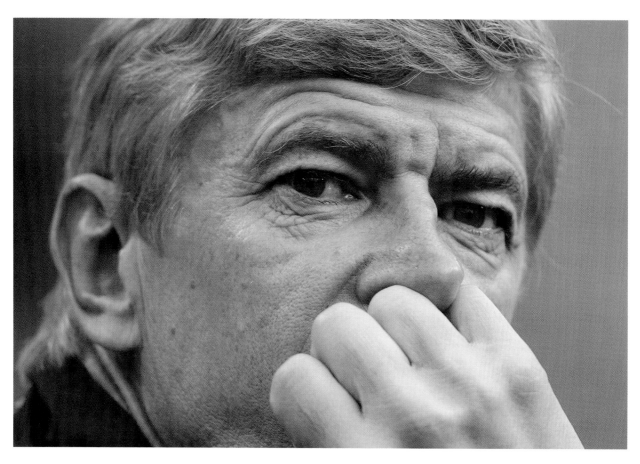

Opposite Emmanuel Adebayor, Johan Djourou and Alex Song did not feature in the inaugural Emirates Cup but they did watch the football. As did the Austrian police when Arsenal visited Salzburg.

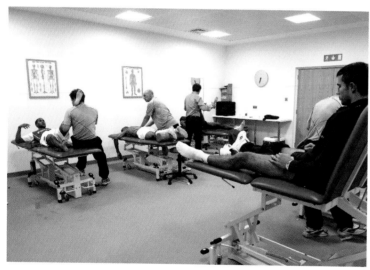

The move to Emirates Stadium has created space for a bigger physio room and allowed the creation of a warm-up area where the players can get a feel of the ball before they go out on to the pitch.

Fans from all over Europe come to Arsenal's Austrian training camp. Occasionally they are able to watch the sessions from a small stand at the ground.

'These two days of the
Emirates Cup are about
playing together, getting
your fitness back and giving
good football to the fans.'

ROBIN VAN PERSIE

The Emirates Cup was held for the first time in 2007 and it is set to become an annual event. Arsenal took the inaugural trophy and Alex Hleb put it to good use.

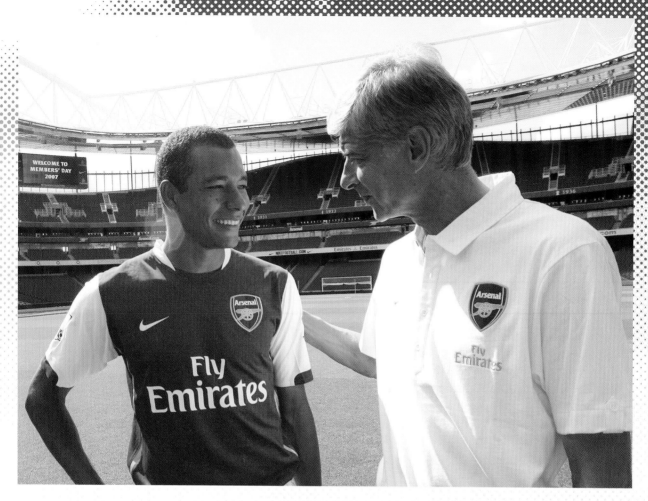

Arsène Wenger takes his media duties seriously. In pre-season, they can range from posing for pictures at Emirates Stadium on photocall day to post-match interviews in Austria.

WORK AND PLAY

Football teams are like swans – for all their grace and panache on the surface, there is an awful lot of hard work going on underneath.

It is always fun, of course. Most little boys grow up with ambitions of becoming a footballer and the ones who have become professionals with Arsenal Football Club are among the best in the world. But the very drive and determination that has enabled them to reach those dizzy heights is an ingrained part of their character. They will compete whether it is a supposedly friendly game of pre-match keepie-uppie or a goal-line 50-50 in the final minute of a deadlocked FA Cup-tie. And training is no exception.

This chapter aims to give you an insight into the demanding environment Arsène Wenger creates for his side. The manager professes to be happiest on the training pitch and employs a plethora of support staff to ensure his sessions are focused yet unpressured.

There is time for a little rest and relaxation too. For example, we'll see Robin van Persie playing table tennis and Emmanuel Adebayor taking on all-comers on the pool table. But if you are thinking these are 'friendlies' then you will be sadly disappointed.

Warm-ups often involve good-humoured games. One of these is volleyball. However, in this version, the players cannot use their hands. That includes Manuel Almunia.

'We have been playing together for a few years. That makes a difference in the game because we all know each other – if I pass to Cesc he knows exactly where the forwards will be.'

GILBERTO

Equipment manager Paul Johnson confers with fitness coach Tony Colbert about the requirements for upcoming training sessions. Paul is also responsible for the team's travel arrangements for away games.

The association between Boro Primorac and Arsène Wenger goes back well over ten years. The Bosnian-born coach had a successful playing career with Yugoslavia before coaching in top-flight French football.

'I play for Arsenal. I am not a tennis player who does it on their own, I am a football player in a team and we achieve things together.'

ROBIN VAN PERSIE

Kolo Toure is not known for his tricks and flicks but the centre back is versatile. During his Arsenal career he has played every position across the defence and midfield.

Lukasz Fabianski and Eduardo arrived at Arsenal in the summer of 2007. Members Day at Emirates Stadium helped them get accustomed to their new surroundings and new team-mates.

Arsenal get many, many requests for signed shirts and footballs. In order to satisfy as many people as possible, they are laid out at the Training Ground for the players to autograph.

'I've been lucky that since I was young I always had big pressure. I don't think about what people think of me or what they expect.'

CESC FABREGAS

Craig Gant helps William Gallas stretch off at the end of a training session. He doubles up as Assistant Fitness Coach and a first-team masseur.

'When I came to Arsenal I was a bit of an individual. But the boss taught me slowly how to play together. You get more out of your career when you work together.'

ROBIN VAN PERSIE

Left Pat Rice is approaching 45 years service at Arsenal as player and coach. In his time he was a tough tackling right-back, a little like Justin Hoyte.

Stretching has always been essential to Arsène Wenger's footballing philosophy. A concentration on diet, rest and shorter, focused sessions also help the manager get the most from his squad.

'My life changed a little bit when I joined Arsenal. I found people like Arsenal so much and the fans stop me in the streets more these days. It is unbelievable.'

WILLIAM GALLAS

Lukasz Fabianski arrived from Legia Warsaw in the summer of 2007. His work in pre-season was seen in the Carling Cup and the final few games of the campaign that followed.

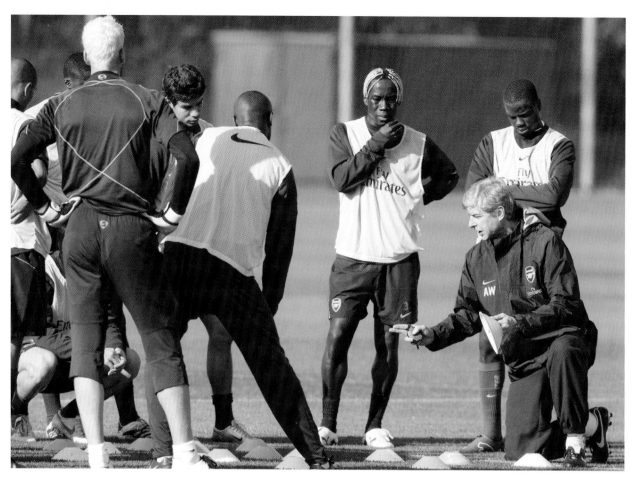

Arsène Wenger conducts training sessions with a stopwatch in his hands. The aim is to make them sharp and intense.

'Even before I was a captain
I thought about being a coach –
but only for the young players.
It is really difficult for a manager
after a defeat and I don't want
to put pressure on my family.'

WILLIAM GALLAS

Goalkeepers do some of their work away from the main group. Coach Gerry Peyton said, 'Keepers are specialised with their training. There is a lot of work on power, handling and concentration. But I still like my keepers to be included in the first team unit.'

'I want to be an Arsenal player. You never know what can happen in football but I am going to knuckle down, train hard, work hard and perform when I get my chance.'

JUSTIN HOYTE

Mannequins and bounce boards are regularly used in training drills at Arsenal.

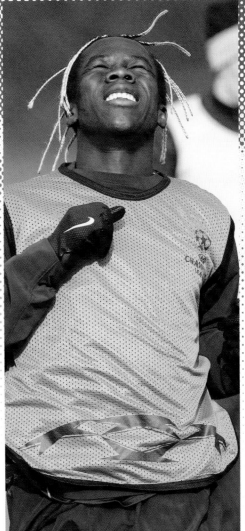

Before his departure to Milan, Mathieu Flamini was known for his physical fitness at Arsenal. Statistics proved he covered much more ground per game than the average midfielder.

Tomas Rosicky and Abou Diaby try their hands at photography in Amsterdam while Gael Clichy and Theo Walcott share a DVD on the plane home from the Dutch capital.

THE CLUB

There is one team at Arsenal Football Club who have been performing at the top of their game – week in, week out – for decades ... The Board.

While Arsène Wenger may have fully supported the construction of a new ground and training complex since 1999, it was the Club's directors who actually made it happen. The impressive, award-winning Emirates Stadium was on time, on budget and has quickly become 'home' despite 93 years at Highbury. However, perhaps the Training Ground was just as important for the Club because it enabled Wenger to create his footballing vision at Arsenal.

Unsurprisingly, this chapter spends most of its time in those two places. At the Training Ground, the gym, boot room and restaurant give you the inside track on Wenger's 'football factory'. While at the stadium, you get a peek at the Annual General Meeting and pitch preparation.

However, the Club has hardly rested on its laurels since these major buildings went up. During the second season of the 'Emirates Era', the Club invested in a huge indoor pitch at the Training Ground and introduced a television station. You'll see those too.

Of course, Arsenal already have one of the most popular football club websites in the world and this chapter shows you a player using that medium to talk directly to supporters.

For a club with long traditions, Arsenal have always moved with the times.

'He acquires young players that most people have never heard of. But he develops them, he supports them and coaches them. He has really worked miracles with the squad.'

CHAIRMAN PETER HILL-WOOD

Keith Edelman — Peter Hill-Wood — Daniel Fiszman

Arsenal's Annual General Meeting was held at the Woolwich Suite at Emirates Stadium. The Board of Directors and shareholders are in attendance to hear the Club's financial results announced and explained.

'A lot of players are saying "Oh, I have to be the top-scorer". But for me the first thing is to play football. There is lots of responsibility because you are playing in front of 60,000 people.'

ROBIN VAN PERSIE

Pitch preparation starts well before matchday. But the grass is watered before the game and is cut afterwards.

The content and layout of the Arsenal Training ground were almost entirely decided by Arsène Wenger and his backroom staff. Apart from players and coaches, 24 staff are based there.

'Arsenal has something different from other clubs. We have built something really special. The players change but we can always play good football.'

KOLO TOURE

The Training Centre has six changing rooms, a steamroom, a gym, treatment rooms, massage baths and a restaurant.

Head Chef Rob Fagg prepares healthy food for the players each day including meat, fish, pasta, vegetables and an extensive salad selection.

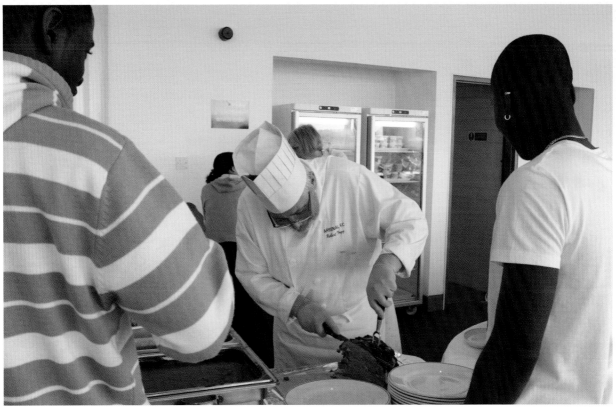

'In England when there is a problem, people say "you have to buy". But you have to consider the development of your players internally as well'

ARSÈNE WENGER

'George Allison was manager for 13 years in the 1930s and 1940s but by 2011 Arsène will have been with us nearly 15 years. That's a remarkable performance.'

PETER HILL-WOOD

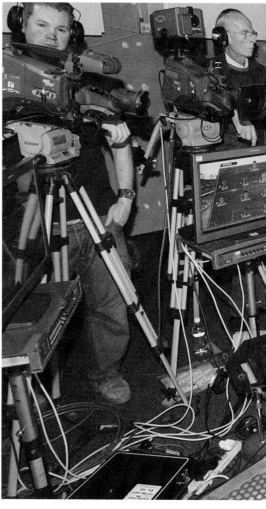

Left The launch night of Arsenal TV in January 2008 saw a discussion show held in the press conference room at Emirates Stadium.
The panel was Arsène Wenger, Ray Parlour, Martin Keown and comedian Matt Lucas.
The host was Des Lynam.

William Gallas held a live webchat on Arsenal.com in October 2007. Over 3000 e-mails came in with questions for the Frenchman and he spent over an hour answering as many of them as he could.

MATCHDAY

This will be the highlight or lowlight of the week. It is what players prepare for and supporters anticipate. If football is a religion then this is its day of worship – and the congregation can hardly be more devoted. These pictures show the pre-match preparations at Emirates Stadium, the build-up to kick-off and after the final whistle.

Footballers and football fans love their rituals before a game. For the player this is maybe putting on one boot first or going out of the tunnel last while for the follower it could be wearing a lucky scarf or buying the programme from the same seller. Whatever. It is familiarity that breeds the contented football person and this chapter aims to capture the flavour of matchday on and off the pitch.

The move from Highbury was only a matter of half-a-mile but it was a massive leap forward in the Club's operation. On matchday, the preparations are paramount and these exclusive shots give you the inside track on what that entails. From the box office to the mascot to the stewards controlling the arrival of the team bus. They are the teams that ultimately help THE team.

In fact you could say they control all the ingredients of a successful matchday – barring the result of course.

'The opening games at Emirates Stadium were like a first night at the theatre. Outwardly everybody wanted to appear calm but everyone was on edge and the adrenalin was flowing to make sure everything went well.'

DIRECTOR KEN FRIAR

The players are bussed from the Training Ground to Emirates Stadium and arrive around 90 minutes before kick-off.

The ticket office at Emirates Stadium is always busy before a game. It is not surprising given that its average Premier League attendance was more than 60,000 in its opening two seasons.

'We are a young side but remember the life of this team started years ago. We are used to playing in big pressure and in a big atmosphere.'

ARSÈNE WENGER

On the eve of away games in the Champions League, Arsène Wenger
holds a press conference. Normally it is held at the opposition ground.
This one was at the San Siro ahead of the 2-0 win against Milan.

Opposite Two Champions League traditions can be seen here – the flying of the 'star ball' banner in the centre circle and, on the big screens, the two sets of players shaking hands.

'It is not my song. It is the song of the players. I asked if we could play [a Timbaland track] when we did the warm-up on my pitch. When they hear that song they are focused. It gives them some energy.'

WILLIAM GALLAS

Arsenal have a mascot home and away. This is Joshua Ryan, aged 7, with Cesc Fabregas before the Premier League game at West Ham in September 2007.

'When I am on the pitch I really enjoy myself, and this is so important for a player. I'm not sure if I could play in a team which played long balls all the time.'

CESC FABREGAS

This is the night time view of Emirates Stadium from the balcony of the Boardroom. It was situated in the East Stand at Highbury but, when Arsenal moved, it was taken apart and reassembled in exactly the same way on the top floor of Highbury House, the Club's administrative offices.

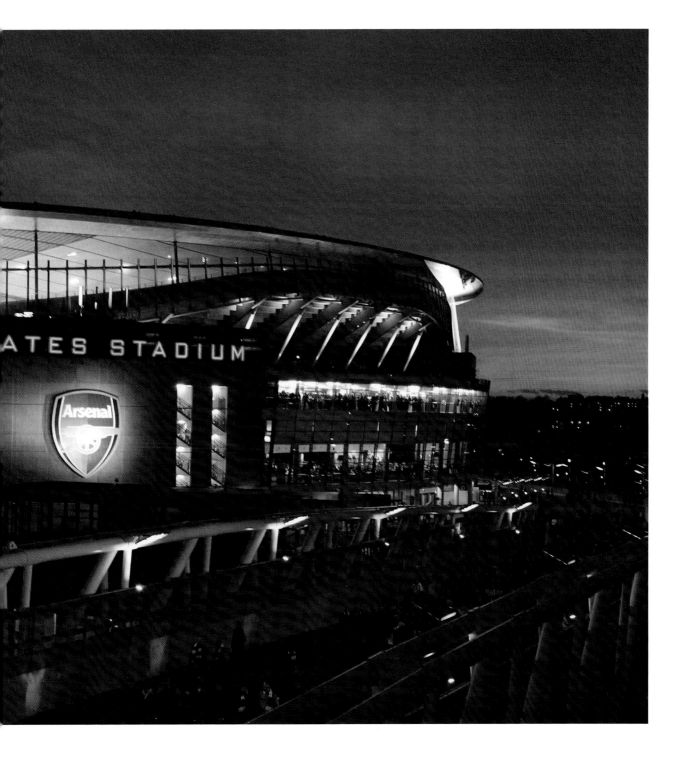

ON AND OFF THE PITCH

Football's focus is always on the pitch. Players and coaches work tirelessly to perform well on it, the groundsmen work tirelessly to prepare it and the Club works tirelessly to ensure everyone's watching experience is first class. That is why supporters work tirelessly all week so they can buy tickets.

This chapter concentrates on the events on and off the pitch around kick-off. It is a highly charged couple of hours for everybody involved, so these will be perhaps the most expressive pictures contained within the book.

The positives range from the youthful enthusiasm of the matchday mascot to the elation of scoring a goal. The negatives will reflect everything from the anguish of a spurned opportunity to the utter dismay after Eduardo's horrific injury at Birmingham City in February 2008.

These pictures also convey the emotion in the stands and the near hysteria an important moment can cause to the characters who congregate there each week.

You might not realise it from this chapter but, even at the top clubs in the 21st century, football is still a game at heart. Every professional player began their involvement purely because they enjoyed it and, even for the most committed fan, the sport can be classed as a 'serious pleasure'. It is not called the 'world's game' for nothing and, for those in its grasp, nothing matches the passions it can rouse.

'I just love to play those games when the fans are on top of you, and every piece of action gets them involved. It's great to be a part of that.'

ROBIN VAN PERSIE

Robin van Persie salutes the crowd ahead of the home game with Manchester City in August 2007. He is about to line-up with his team-mates for the Premier League anthem, which was introduced at the start of the previous season.

'We have a very young squad but we're not scared of anything and want to win things.'

CESC FABREGAS

'I don't remember the incident very well and it is not something that I want to see again on television or in the newspapers.'

EDUARDO

This was a key point of Arsenal's 2007/08 season. On 23 February Birmingham's Martin Taylor challenges Eduardo. The tackle is mistimed but not malicious yet it fractures his leg and dislocates his ankle.

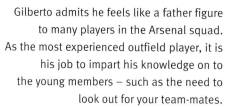

Gilberto admits he feels like a father figure to many players in the Arsenal squad. As the most experienced outfield player, it is his job to impart his knowledge on to the young members – such as the need to look out for your team-mates.

Right This picture, taken from the top of the East Stand at Emirates Stadium, shows the Arsenal players mobbing William Gallas after his goal against Chelsea in December 2007. It was a crucial strike against a major opponent, that is why every outfield player is either congratulating him or in the process of reaching their captain.

Gael Clichy is a firm favourite with the Arsenal fans and was runner-up in the Player of the Season poll for 2007/08.

'Football is not about age. It's not about money. Football is about if you want to run for each other, if you want to fight for each other and if you want to really play some ball.'

ROBIN VAN PERSIE

Robin van Persie battles his way past Blackburn's Ryan Nelsen in February 2008. The Dutchman enjoys a fine record against the Lancashire side and came to prominence for Arsenal with two goals in the FA Cup Semi-final between the two sides in 2005.

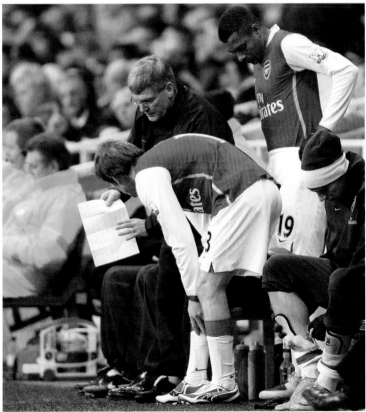

Physio Gary Lewin left Arsenal in June 2008 to join the England set-up on a full-time basis. He originally came to the Club as a goalkeeper but, after studying at Guy's Hospital in London, returned as part of the medical team in 1983.

A couple of faces in the crowd: Captain America (Theo Walcott's dad) flexes his muscles during the home game against Birmingham in January 2008 while a substituted Cesc Fabregas spots someone he knows.

'Football can change your life in one second. At the start of the season, I was not playing. But football changed my life again and now I have signed a new contract. I am one of the happiest men around.'

MANUEL ALMUNIA

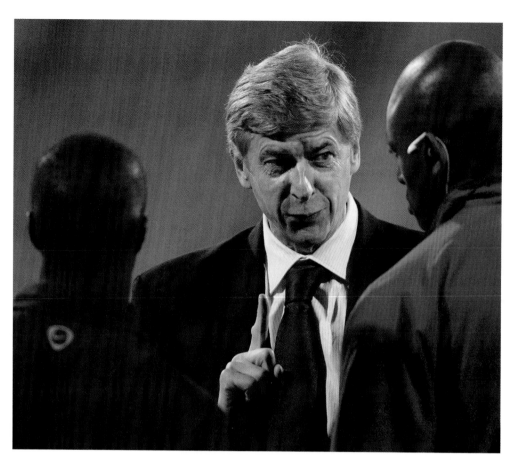

Arsène Wenger gets his point across to Abou Diaby ahead of the Champions League tie at Steaua Bucharest in October 2007. The well-manned bench from that game is also pictured.

'The secret is to believe in yourself. That is the message I always say. No matter what happens, or what others say, you must believe in yourself and work hard.'

EMMANUEL ADEBAYOR

'When Cesc was a young boy he scored goals. That's a nice disease to have. Sometimes it disappears but it always comes back when you are a mature player.'

ARSÈNE WENGER

'We are ready for European competition at the highest level. I believe in this team.'

TOMAS ROSICKY

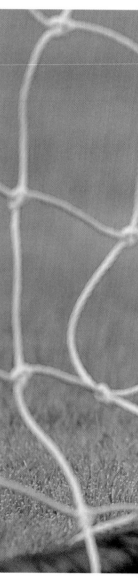

Champions League nights have a different feel on and off the pitch. The 'star' branding is used on the ball and all around the ground, while the fanfare surrounding the pre-match line-up is a valuable way to build the atmosphere.

TEAM SPIRIT

Team spirit is the mortar of any football side. You can gather together as many big strong bricks as you want but if there is nothing to bind them together then you do not have a team, merely a collection of individuals.

When signing a player, Arsène Wenger always says he considers two factors – their technical quality and their spirit. The first can be assessed relatively easily on the training pitch but the second is harder to pin down. It is their character, their humour, their determination and the way they mix with others.

In fact the only time team spirit can be truly identified is when a side is going through tough times. The skill of a manager is to blend the different personalities in his side into a unit that is stronger than the sum of its parts – and steadfastly refuses to lose.

This chapter aims to capture the spirit within the Arsenal camp. These are the spontaneous moments when the team are acting on their instincts whether they are to laugh, to cry, to celebrate, be respectful or be focused. On these occasions the team comes together in the most natural way – and the spirit is there for all to see.

'Who is the biggest joker in the squad? Well I'm not too bad. Sometimes I have a laugh with some players. Alex Song and Bacary Sagna do that too.'

WILLIAM GALLAS

Manuel Almunia is buried beneath this pile of players. The Arsenal goalkeeper won the 'Crossbar Challenge' held for French television at the Training Ground at the end of the summer in 2007. He was the only member of the squad to hit the woodwork from the halfway line.

Emmanuel Adebayor and Bacary Sagna play
an impromptu game of keepie-uppie in the
reception area at the Training Ground.
Their celebrations are on the next page.

First-team players amuse themselves in the tunnel after their Carling Cup counterparts had beaten Newcastle United at Emirates Stadium in late 2007.

'I just ignore all the attention [in the media] because you might hear stuff you don't want to hear as well as stuff you do. All the top players at Arsenal have told me to do that.'

THEO WALCOTT

The bench is forced to group together for warmth at Slavia Prague in November 2007. It was a cold, wet night in the Czech capital, but the goalless draw was enough to put Arsenal into the Knockout Stages of the Champions League.

'The huddle happened after the first game of the 2007/08 season against Fulham when we won in the last minute. The pressure was on our shoulders and we were just so happy. Now we do it after every game.'

WILLIAM GALLAS

'As a captain William reminds me a bit of Patrick Vieira; he's an experienced, older player and he knows how to talk to us.'

GAEL CLICHY

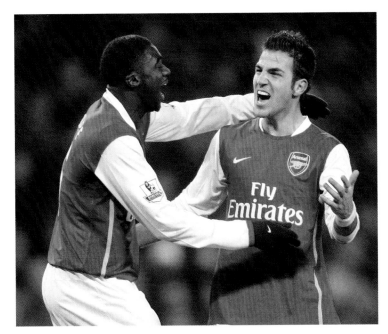

William Gallas was given the captain's armband at the start of the 2007/08 season. One of his innovations was to request the same song be played at the start of each game at Emirates Stadium. It is 'The way I are' by Timbaland.

'Sometimes people don't realise but it's like a family here. I know I'm in a big club with great players, some great friends and a great manager.'

CESC FABREGAS

CELEBRATIONS

Arsène Wenger's Arsenal have always made football appear effortless. Scoring goals has rarely seemed to be a big problem. A patter of passes followed by a precise finish – simple really. However, having hit the net, the team's celebrations always betray them. That explosion of emotion suggests their goals are the culmination of technique, tenacity and tireless hard work. Nothing that comes so easily is worth celebrating so hard.

This section focuses on those celebrations – from the crowd, from the bench and from the team. In the 2007/08 season there was little to compare with the crucial injury-time strike against Manchester United or that historic and thoroughly deserved 2-0 victory at Milan.

These pictures prove it.

Some celebrations are amusing or personal. For example, the following few pages will show how Emmanuel Adebayor's effervescent character shines through when he scores a goal while, in one shot, Theo Walcott points to the sky to remember a loved one.

However, most celebrations are merely a connection between the crowd and the players. In almost all of these pictures, the scorer runs to the fans. His team-mates might follow him, but the primary aim is to fuel himself with the applause of the supporters.

'I never set a target. I could say I want to score 30, and in March, if I have scored 30, what am I going to do? Am I going to stop?'

EMMANUEL ADEBAYOR

Nicklas Bendtner slides towards the fans after his strike against Newcastle United in September 2007. It was the Dane's first competitive goal for Arsenal.

'For me, the most important thing is to create goals. The feeling you get when you score is amazing but I have been educated since I was very young to make assists and make the team play.'

CESC FABREGAS

One of the more elaborate celebrations of recent years. Emmanuel Adebayor shines Mathieu Flamini's boots after his rasping effort against Newcastle United in September 2007.

'This is a unique team in Europe because, as we say in Holland, the nose is pointed in the same direction.'

ROBIN VAN PERSIE

Opposite Robin van Persie takes flight after his scorching free-kick against Sunderland in 2007.

'I am not here to say whether I am as good as Drogba or Inzaghi. The most important thing for me is to keep on getting goals and playing my part on the pitch.'

EMMANUEL ADEBAYOR

Emmanuel Adebayor goes behind the
advertising boards on New Year's Day 2008.

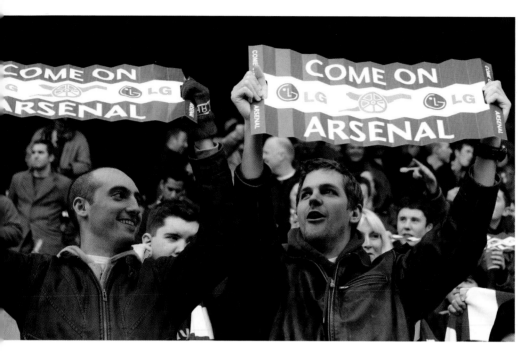

This is a picture of relief more than celebration. Wigan held Arsenal at bay for 83 minutes at Emirates Stadium in November 2007. Then William Gallas broke the deadlock.

'When I signed for Arsenal I always wanted to give my best. Then I was made captain and now to give my best is to lift a trophy.'

WILLIAM GALLAS

Arsène Wenger can get involved in goal celebrations though he sometimes has little choice. William Gallas and Cesc Fabregas both ran to their manager after their crucial late strikes against Manchester United and Milan in the 2007/08 season.

'There was never any doubt that we were going to come out strongly that night in Milan. Whatever we had to do, we were going to do it.'

PHILIPPE SENDEROS

The team rightly salute the fans after one of the Club's best ever wins in Europe – the 2-0 victory at Milan in 2007/08.